Florence Nightingale

A Buddy Book
by
Sarah Tieck

ABDO
Publishing Company

VISIT US AT
www.abdopublishing.com

Published by ABDO Publishing Company, 4940 Viking Drive, Suite 622, Edina, Minnesota 55435. Copyright © 2007 by Abdo Consulting Group, Inc. International copyrights reserved in all countries. No part of this book may be reproduced in any form without written permission from the publisher.

Printed in the United States.

Contributing Editor: Michael P. Goecke
Graphic Design: Jane Halbert
Cover Photograph: Library of Congress
Interior Photographs/Illustrations: Library of Congress, Getty Images

Library of Congress Cataloging-in-Publication Data

Tieck, Sarah, 1976–
   Florence Nightingale / Sarah Tieck.
     p. cm. — (First biographies. Set V)
   Includes index.
   ISBN 10 1-59679-786-X
   ISBN 13   978-1-59679-786-4
   1. Nightingale, Florence, 1820–1910—Juvenile literature. 2. Nurses Juvenile literature.—
England—Biography I. Title II. Series: Gosda, Randy T, 1959– . First Biographies. Set V.

RT37.N5T54 2006
610.73092—dc22

                                           2005031969

Table Of Contents

Who Is Florence Nightingale?

Florence Nightingale was a famous nurse and writer. She helped change medicine.

Florence Nightingale lived in Great Britain during Victorian times. At this time, most women didn't have jobs. Many people believed that women could not do certain things. Florence proved these people wrong.

Because of Florence Nightingale, many women became nurses. She helped make hospitals better.

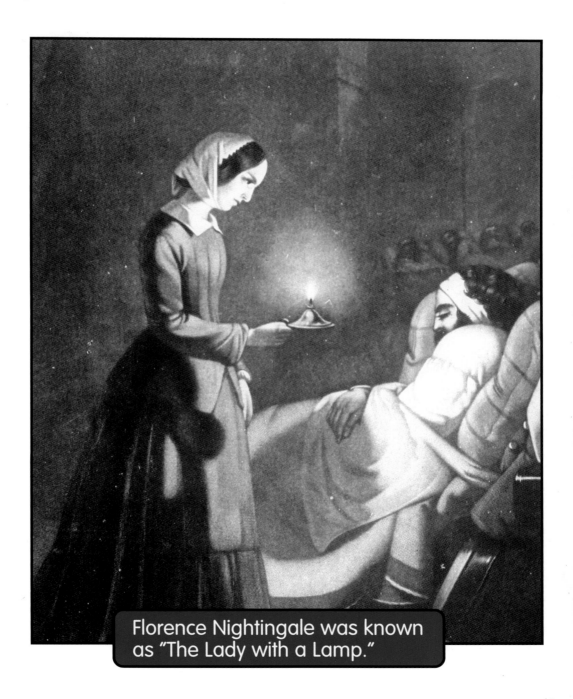

Florence Nightingale was known as "The Lady with a Lamp."

Florence's Family

Florence Nightingale was born on May 12, 1820. Florence was named after Florence, Italy. This is the city where she was born.

Florence's mother was Frances Nightingale. Some people called Frances "Fanny." Florence's father was William Nightingale. Florence had an older sister named Parthenope.

A portrait of Florence.

Florence's family was wealthy and lived in England. Florence and Parthenope were born when their parents were traveling around Europe. William and Fanny were on a very long trip after their wedding.

Growing Up

There are many stories about Florence as a child.

She grew up in the country at a house called Embley. In the summer, the Nightingales went to a house called Lea Hurst. They also traveled to London, England, and other places in Europe.

The Nightingales had many servants and workers to help take care of the house. Florence and Parthenope had a governess to take care of them.

A view of Embley.

Florence loved to learn. Florence's mother taught her how to run a household.

Florence's father helped her learn history, philosophy, and mathematics. Florence was good at mathematics. Florence's father also taught her Greek, Latin, French, German, and Italian.

A Special Calling

When she was 16, Florence said she got a calling from God to do something important with her life. At first she wasn't sure what she was supposed to do. At 25, she realized she wanted to be a nurse and help other people.

Around this time, men started asking Florence to marry them. Florence said no to all of them. Florence wanted to be a nurse.

It would take many years before Florence became a nurse.

Florence's mother and sister were not happy. They thought Florence should get married. Many women Florence's age became wives.

Becoming A Nurse

Florence wanted to be a nurse more than anything. But in Florence's time, nursing was not considered a proper job for a girl. People believed it wasn't safe. People also worried that nurses would get sick or hurt, too. This is why Florence's parents wouldn't let her go to nursing school.

Florence wasn't going to give up. She decided to learn everything she could on her own. She taught herself about nursing and cleanliness.

A drawing of young Florence.

Florence waited for many years. Finally when she turned 31, her father said she could train to be a nurse. She went to school in Kaiserswerth, Germany. There, she studied at the Institute for Protestant Deaconesses.

After she was done with school, Florence went to work as a nurse. Her first job was at a hospital for women in London. It was called The Establishment for Gentlewomen During Illness.

Florence working with a patient.

Going To War

The Crimean War began in March 1853. The war started because the country of Russia invaded part of the Ottoman Empire. Today, the Ottoman Empire is known as Turkey. Soldiers from Great Britain and France went to help.

Many British soldiers got sick or hurt during the fighting. Some soldiers got diseases like cholera and malaria.

RUSSIA

GREAT
BRITAIN

UKRAINE

Crimea
Region

FRANCE

Scutari

TURKEY

Crimea used to be part of the Ottoman
Empire. Today, Crimea is part of Ukraine.

Florence wanted to help the soldiers. The government sent Florence with 38 other nurses. Some people didn't like that Florence was helping. Still, Florence and the nurses went to a hospital in Scutari.

Florence was surprised when she got to Scutari. The army hospital was very dirty. The men didn't have blankets or food. Most had not had baths. Many were wearing dirty clothes. Some had become even sicker or died because of the hospital conditions.

Many soldiers were hurt in battles.
Florence and the nurses helped them.

Florence knew that cleanliness helped people heal. She worked to clean the hospital and to help the soldiers heal.

Sometimes, Florence would walk around the hospital at night with a lamp. She checked on the soldiers. People started calling her "The Lady with a Lamp."

Florence wanted to prove that nursing was a good job for women. She made sure the nurses were safe. They stayed together and Florence watched over them. She had many rules.

Florence carrying her famous lamp.

People noticed that many men were getting healthy. Because of Florence, people were starting to think nursing was a good job for women.

Coming Home

In 1856, Florence returned to England. Some people called her a hero. They were glad that she had helped England in the war. Florence got many awards for her hard work as a nurse.

Florence had many ideas about how to improve medicine. She talked to Queen Victoria and Prince Albert. Also, she shared her stories with the 1857 Royal Commission on the Health of the Army. Florence's ideas led to many positive changes for hospitals and nurses.

A view of the Scutari hospital.

Florence wrote many books and pamphlets. Her most famous was *Notes on Nursing*. This was first published in 1860. *Notes on Nursing* is still published today. Florence asked her friends to help make hospitals better.

Around this time, Florence founded the Nightingale School and Home for Nurses at St. Thomas's Hospital. Florence's school helped train many nurses.

Florence (seated at center) with a group of London nurses.

A Long Life

During the war, Florence had become very sick. She stayed sick for the rest of her life. Because of this, she spent much time in bed. Being sick didn't stop Florence, though. She worked through her whole life.

She did many things to help change hospitals and make them cleaner. She invented a chart to show how many people got sick and how many people healed. People still use charts like this today.

A statue of Florence stands in Waterloo Place, London.

Florence shared her ideas with politicians, writers, and other people. King Edward VII honored Florence's hard work. He gave her the Order of Merit. She was the first woman to receive the award.

Florence Nightingale died at age 90 on August 13, 1910. She was buried near her childhood home.

Many people are still grateful for Florence's hard work and ideas. Today, she is considered the person who started modern nursing.

Edward VII, King of England

Important Dates

May 12, 1820 Florence Nightingale is born in Italy.

1821 The Nightingale family returns to England.

1837 Florence says she gets a calling from God to do something special.

1851 Florence's father says she can go to school to be a nurse. Florence trains in Kaiserswerth, Germany.

1853 Florence gets her first job at The Establishment for Gentlewomen During Illness in London. The Crimean War begins.

1854–56 Florence goes to the Crimean War to help nurse the British soldiers. She cleans the hospital. In 1855, she becomes very sick with Crimean Fever.

1860 Florence publishes *Notes on Nursing*. Also, the Nightingale Training School for Nurses opens.

1907 King Edward VII gives Florence the Order of Merit. She is the first woman to receive this award.

August 13, 1910 Florence Nightingale dies at age 90.

Important Words

calling a person's strong belief that they are supposed to do something.

cleanliness in a neat and tidy way.

governess a woman who is hired to take care of children.

modern the way of life in the present time.

pamphlet a small booklet with a paper cover.

politician someone who is elected to serve in the government.

Victorian life during the time when Queen Victoria ruled England. Victoria was queen from 1837 until her death in 1901.

Web Sites

To learn more about Florence Nightingale, visit ABDO Publishing Company on the World Wide Web. Web site links about Florence Nightingale are featured on our Book Links page. These links are routinely monitored and updated to provide the most current information available.

www.abdopublishing.com

Index